LIKENESS

poems by

Katrina Roberts

Finishing Line Press
Georgetown, Kentucky

LIKENESS

Copyright © 2022 by Katrina Roberts
ISBN 979-8-88838-047-5 First Edition
All rights reserved under International and Pan-American Copyright Conventions.
No part of this book may be reproduced in any manner whatsoever without written permission from the publisher, except in the case of brief quotations embodied in critical articles and reviews.

Also by KATRINA ROBERTS

How Late Desire Looks
The Quick
Friendly Fire
Underdog
Lace

Because You Asked: A Book of Answers
on the Art & Craft of the Writing Life

Publisher: Leah Huete de Maines
Editor: Christen Kincaid
Cover Art: Katrina Roberts
Author Photo; Kimberly Miner
Cover Design: Katrina Roberts

Order online: www.finishinglinepress.com
also available on amazon.com

Author inquiries and mail orders:
Finishing Line Press
P. O. Box 1626
Georgetown, Kentucky 40324
U. S. A.

Table of Contents

Prologue .... *xiii*

I.

[faraday] *1*
[we must rely on lesser circles of protection] *2*
[an island of trash three times the size of france] *3*
[scalene] *4*
[colosseum] *5*
[self-portrait as struck match with promethean vixen] *6*
[surely such a beautiful equation should free even…] *7*
[sobriety suits you] *8*
[self-portrait as early-morning cerberus…] *9*
[anodyne for everything I've neglected to offer] *10*
[superconducting quantum interference devices…] *11*
[algorithms for insecurity of the food sort] *12*
[whether she's guilty of comparative trauma…] *13*
[for whom among us has not felt herself a cipher] *14*
[asemic] *15*
[perks to any club come with a price] *16*
[diary of immeasurable fortune] *17*
[our diagram of ubiquitous sorrow] *18*
[self-portrait as both tenor & vehicle] *19*
[toque pastueño with notation for ultimate sorrow] *20*
[only an ordinance of clouds] *21*
[sanctuary] *22*

II. *(Tangrams)*

[poised to pierce that garment of fog with such nonchalance] 25
["please write back soon, sincerely..."] 26
[if stanzas are rooms, downstairs a bear...] 27
[being tangible, images convey time in dissipating tones] 28
[the pacts he breaks might fell an old-growth forest] 29
[or i could be a sister to the danaïdes, condemned as well...] 30
[how alike we seem and yet how utterly at odds] 31
[perhaps bricolage helps to compose an homage...] 32
[her pet schemes seem to assuage her sense of guilt...] 33
[for whoso gendered nouns, & other inquiries toward solace] 34
[but nero must have plucked a cithara, for the fiddle came to be...] ... 35
[oh, but a single berry might induce a suitable détente] 36
[you claim never to have peered into a mirror to see a cannibal?] 37
[their recipe calls for two cups of snow, whisked with a pinch of
    ashwagandha] 38

III. *(Grace, an Ekphrastic Sequence)*

[you may choose to name us weed or flower...] 41
[but a camel may pass with ease through the eye...] 42
[let us pause to consider whether...] 43
[mycelium, mycelium... the ultimate underworld internet] 44
[dear one, at two minutes to midnight...] 45
[if only a picardy third were tonic for all our woes] 46
[tuck her words into a teapot, steep for years...] 47
[displays of frippery or triumphs of will?] 48
[when we speak of a fine fettle, we do so to note your clean edges} 49
[fruit in a boot] 50
[such an allegory of the gift entreats each to follow their heart] 511
[invisible, intricate, often unsung ossicles] 52
[which concessions are palatable in this light...] 53
["no balm in gilead? no physician?... is there no healing..."] 54
[apparently our swords beaten into plowshares...] 55
[oh, mother dear] 56
[throw for best of three, a dance...] 57

IV.

[memoria]	61
[no pavilion sufficiently vast]	62
[an island of ice recedes before our eyes]	63
[utility may be a fine faith for those no longer seen]	64
[how to rein wilderness, or wilderness reigns?]	65
[little red hoodie heresy]	66
[she holds her pose just long enough…]	67
[church keys or whatever else lets you crack open your belief]	68
[how ornate the fuchsia blossoms, when i tender them some care]	69
[anthem for such portals through which we usher others…]	70
[ekphrasis]	71
[for given this string, i'm dirigible]	72
[how many creatures stitch the depths of loam…]	73
[the geometry of desire]	74
[certainly, something pinioned resides inside, opining…]	75
[where language must always fall short]	76
[diaphora]	77
[tell us again how you know you're right]	78
[there's no elixir like risk]	79
[to embrace the day's glory is not to deny each anguish]	80
[schrödinger]	81
[proof of goodwill's armature]	82
[you take with you exquisite answers to every question unasked]	83
Afterword	*93*

"If prose is a house, poetry is a man on fire running quite fast through it."
—*Anne Carson*

PROLOGUE

No
words.
Blunt force
blew the proverbial
roof off everything she knew.
Silence ticked in corners. Mirrors be-
came windows she climbed through giving
birth to self. Each equation craved a proof in this
stunned world. Every wet morning flung shutters wide
onto the slate wiped clean so she could conceive whomever
she might need to be, to become, now, approximately. Versions,

iterations, semblances. Deconstructed origami heart.
Resemblances, echoes. Part dream? Through arched
galleries, they charted rings, strode, drifted distances
via wings. Feathered, furred, scaled, bare. Assembled
to measure time, weather, death tolls. Ants swarmed
surfaces, deer tottered toward tables, tendrils
tangled to grip fingers, forged cradles, bridges.
Mother, daughter, beyond gen- der. Reflected.
Rendered like a sea's brine-swell, its veneer. Vehicle,
and tenor, she refracted, puddle-shattered, resembled
species lost, or nearly. Drawn to screens, light, holes,
repoussoir, behind curtains, veils, she found archetype,
gesture, trope, treasure, espied love for the scarred,
scared, scored, framed. Multi-faceted. Pasture, page,
skin, each palimpsest the precise key. Stripping bark
from self, she flourished a wand, like *Open Sesame...*

I.

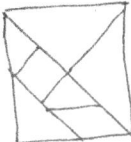

"Her name had the likeness of a name. She had the likeness
of a woman, with hands but no face at all, since she never let herself
see it. She had the likeness of a life, because she was all alone in it.
She lived in the likeness of a house, with walls and a roof and a door
that kept nothing in and nothing out. And when Doll took her up
and swept her away, she had felt a likeness of wings."
—*Marilynne Robinson,* Lila

"In dreams
the body, which longs for transformation
too, suddenly lifts us above the dark
roofs of our houses, and far above

the streets of the town, until they seem
like any other small things fastened to earth."
—*Wesley McNair,* "The Unfastening"

"The missing grew large between them,
Until it pulled the heart right out of the body, until
The drawn heart flew toward the head, flew as a bird flies
Back to its cage and the familiar perch from which it trills.
Then the heart sang in the head, softly at first and then louder,
Sang long and low until the morning light came up over
The school and over the tree, and then the singing stopped…"
—*Bridget Pegeen Kelly,* "Song"

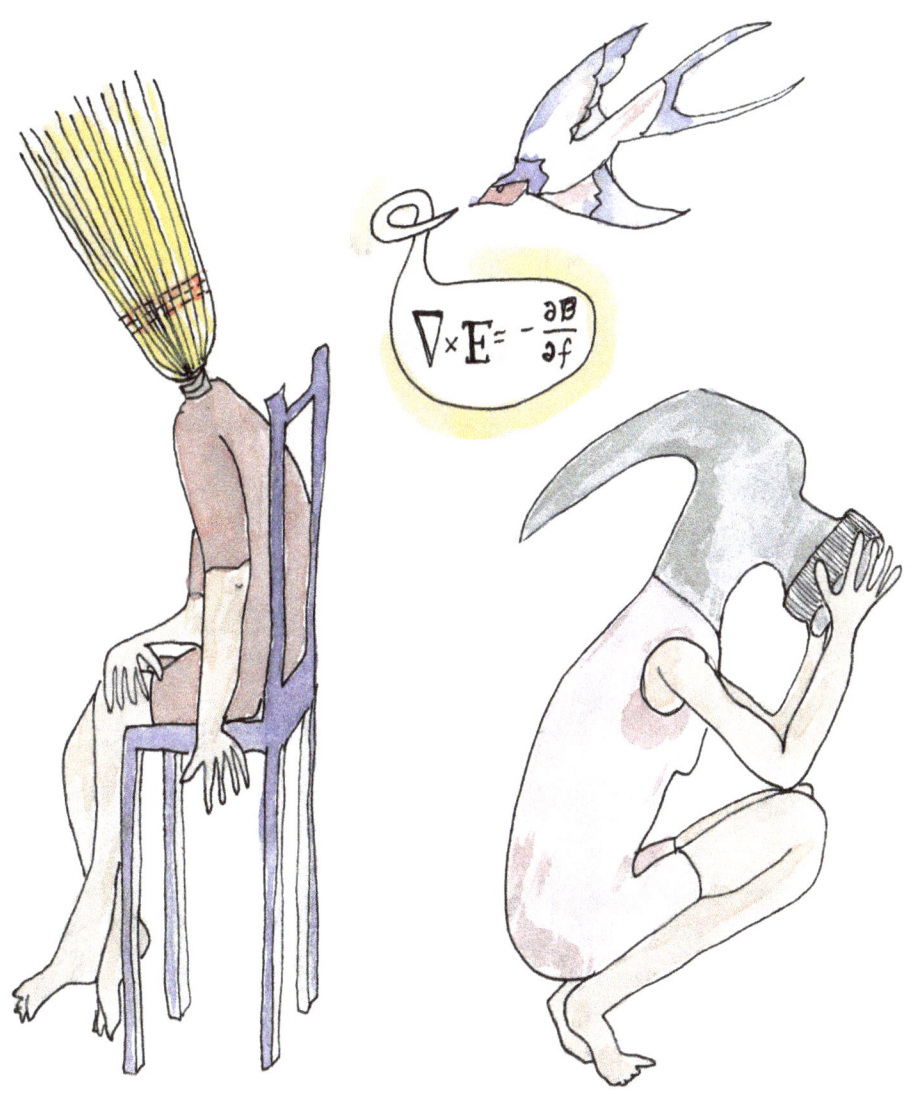

FARADAY

WE MUST RELY on LESSER CIRCLES of PROTECTION

An ISLAND of TRASH THREE TIMES the SIZE of FRANCE

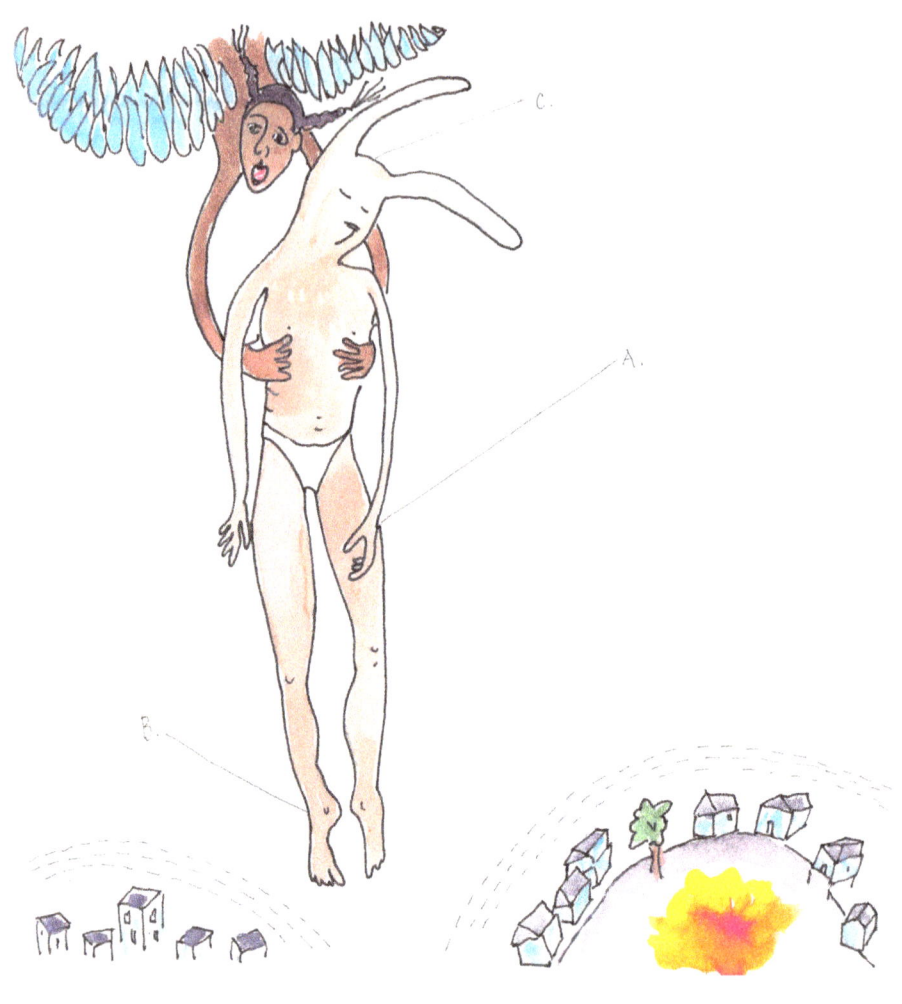

SCALENE

COLOSSEUM

SELF-PORTRAIT as STRUCK MATCH with PROMETHEAN VIXEN

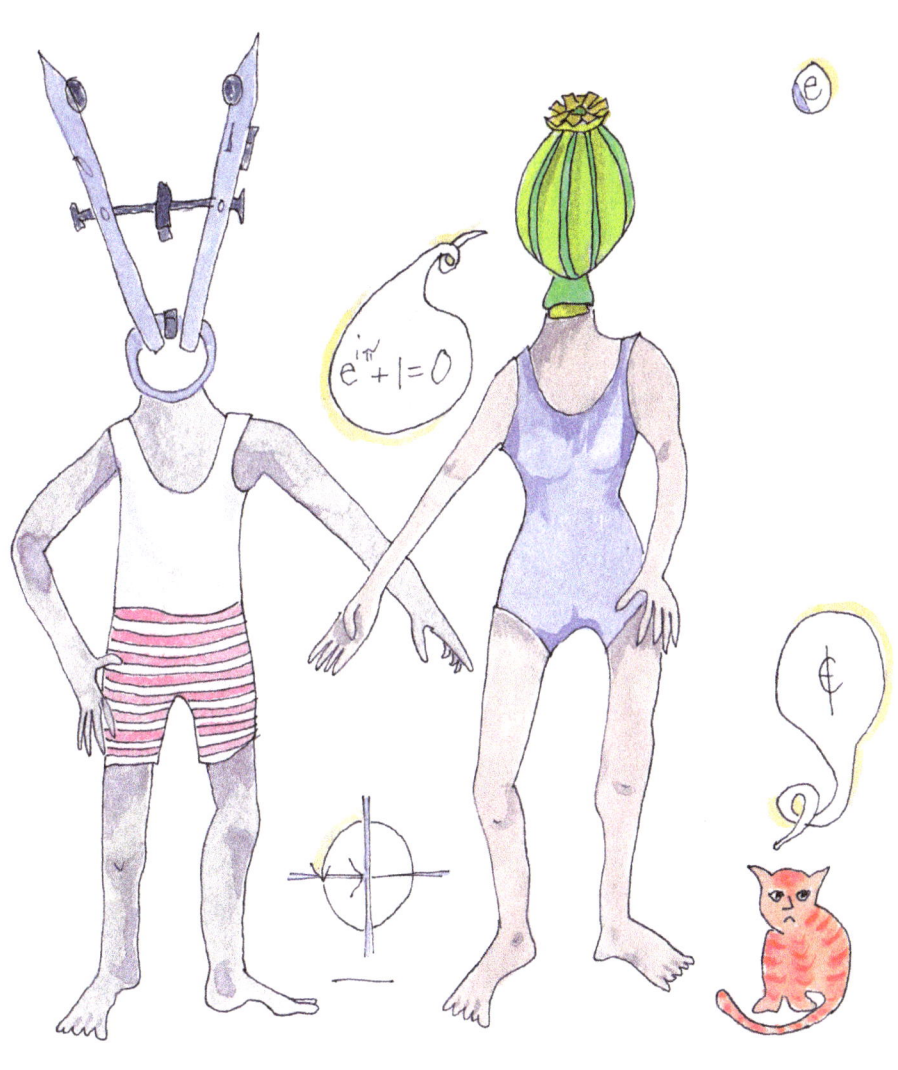

SURELY SUCH a BEAUTIFUL EQUATION SHOULD FREE EVEN the MOST CIRCUMSCRIBED of US
   (—after Euler's Identity)

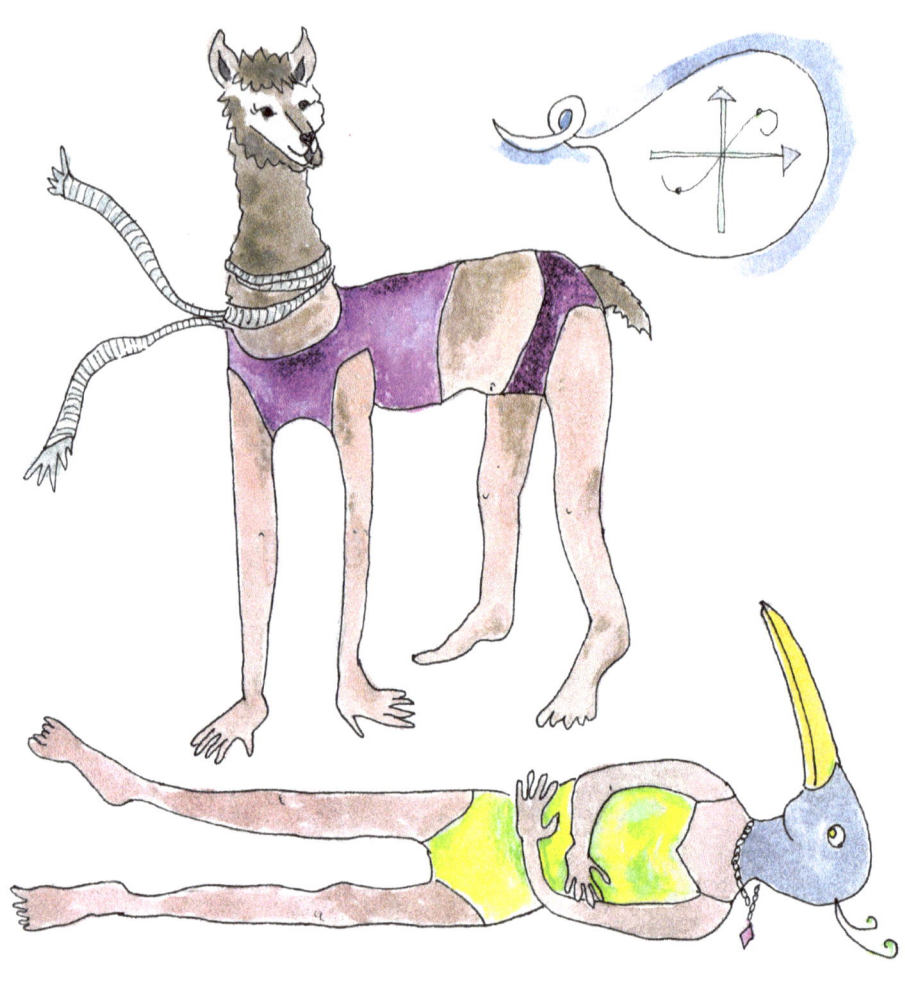

SOBRIETY SUITS YOU

SELF-PORTRAIT as EARLY-MORNING CERBERUS
(—after Antonio Tempesta, ~1606)

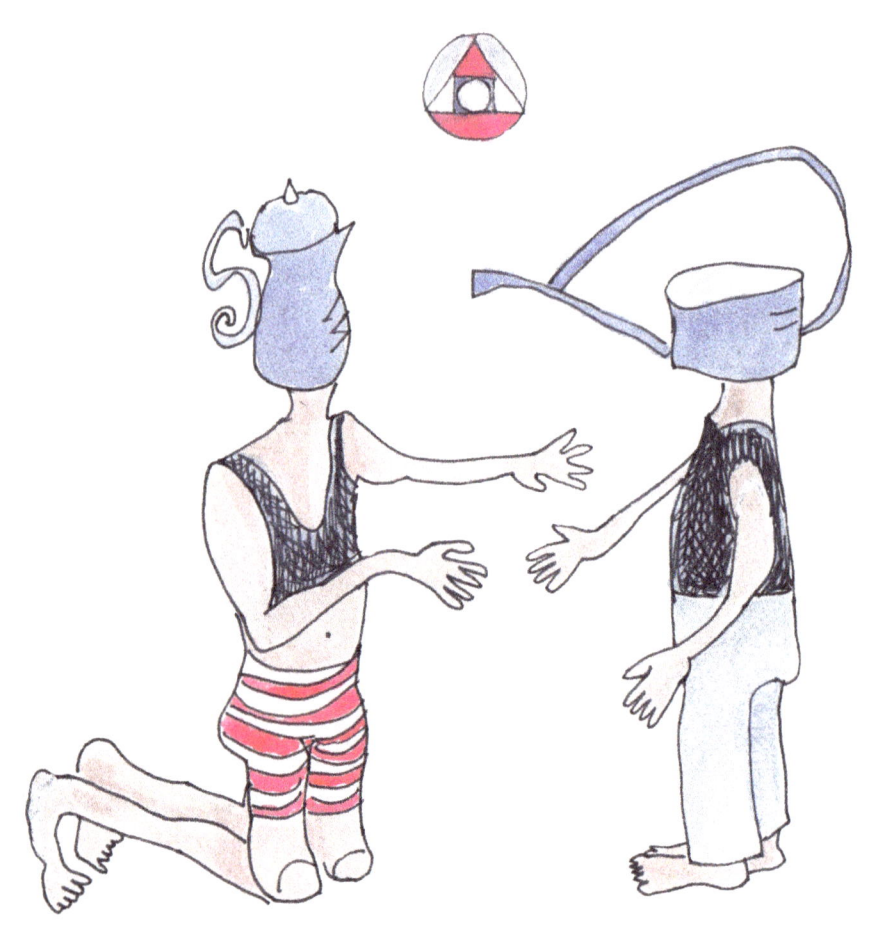

ANODYNE for EVERYTHING I'VE NEGLECTED to OFFER

SUPERCONDUCTING QUANTUM INTERFERENCE DEVICES &
OTHER EMISSARIES of MYSTICISM

ALGORITHMS for INSECURITY of the FOOD SORT

WHETHER SHE'S GUILTY of COMPARATIVE TRAUMA (to the DETRIMENT of the ORIGINAL SPEAKER), IMMINENT EXTINCTION DOESN'T DISTINGUISH

FOR WHOM AMONG US HAS NOT FELT HERSELF a CIPHER?

ASEMIC

PERKS to ANY CLUB COME with a PRICE

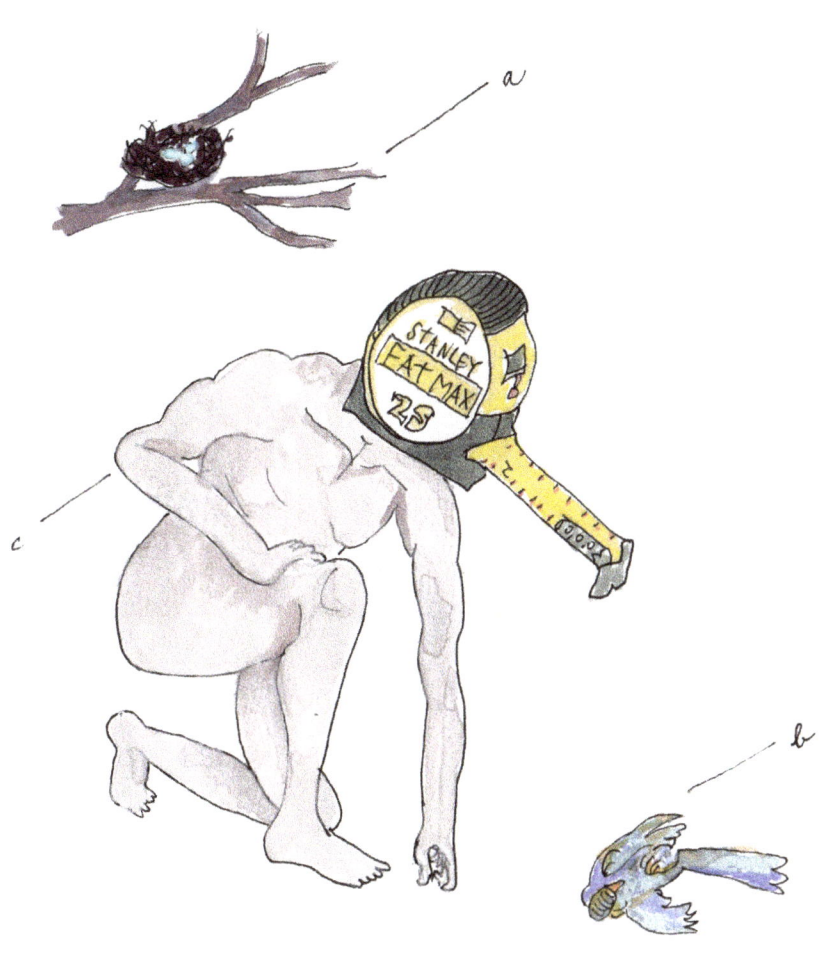

DIARY of IMMEASURABLE FORTUNE

OUR DIAGRAM of UBIQUITOUS SORROW

SELF-PORTRAIT as BOTH TENOR & VEHICLE

TOQUE PASTUEÑO with NOTATION for ULTIMATE SORROW

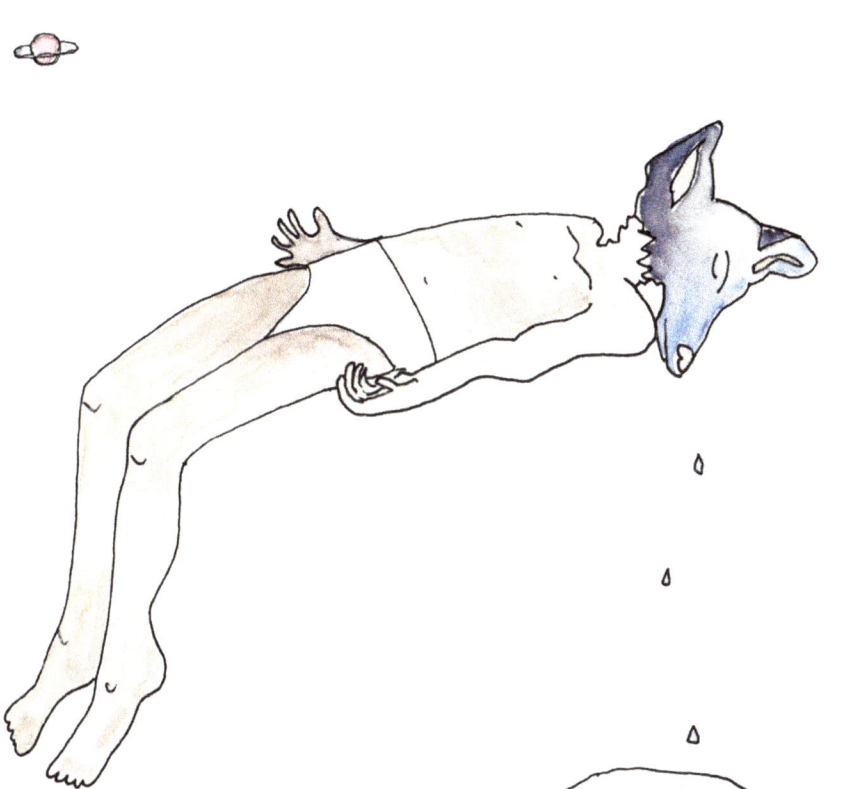

ONLY AN ORDINANCE of CLOUDS

SANCTUARY

II.
(TANGRAMS)

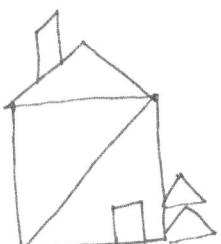

"Go inside a stone
That would be my way.
Let somebody else become a dove
Or gnash with a tiger's tooth…"
—*Charles Simic,* "Stone"

Now I bend over and with my foot turn up a stone,
And there they are: the armies of pale creatures who
Without cease or doubt sew the sweet sad earth.
—*Bridget Pegeen Kelly*, "The Satyr's Heart"

POISED to PIERCE that GARMENT of FOG WORN with SUCH NONCHALANCE

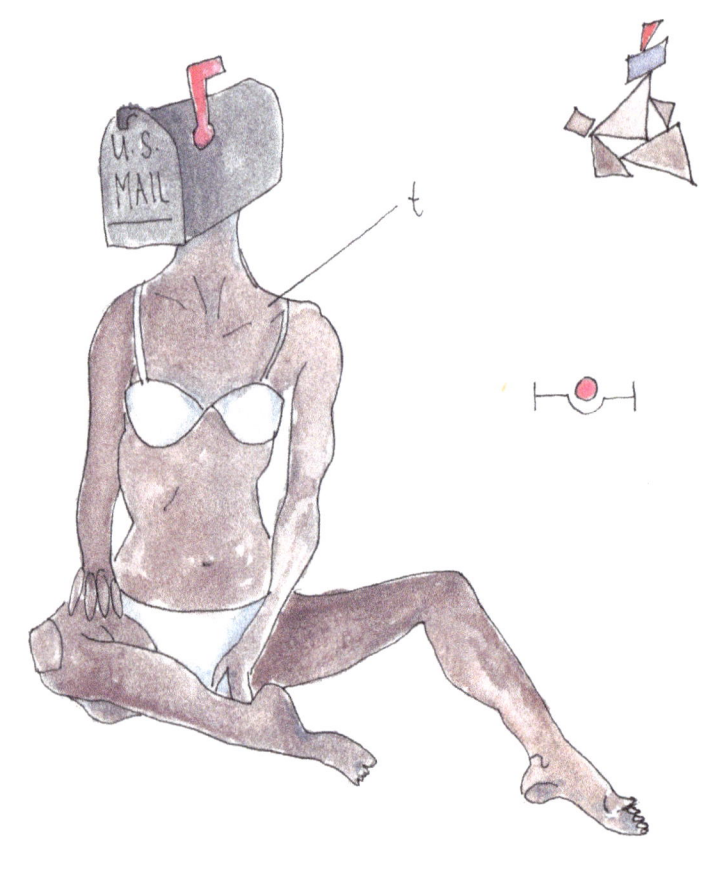

"PLEASE WRITE BACK SOON, SINCERELY…"

IF STANZAS are ROOMS, DOWNSTAIRS a BEAR SNUFFLES CUPBOARDS for BERRIES

BEING TANGLIBLE, IMAGES CONVEY TIME in DISSIPATING TONES

THE PACTS HE BREAKS MIGHT FELL an OLD-GROWTH FOREST

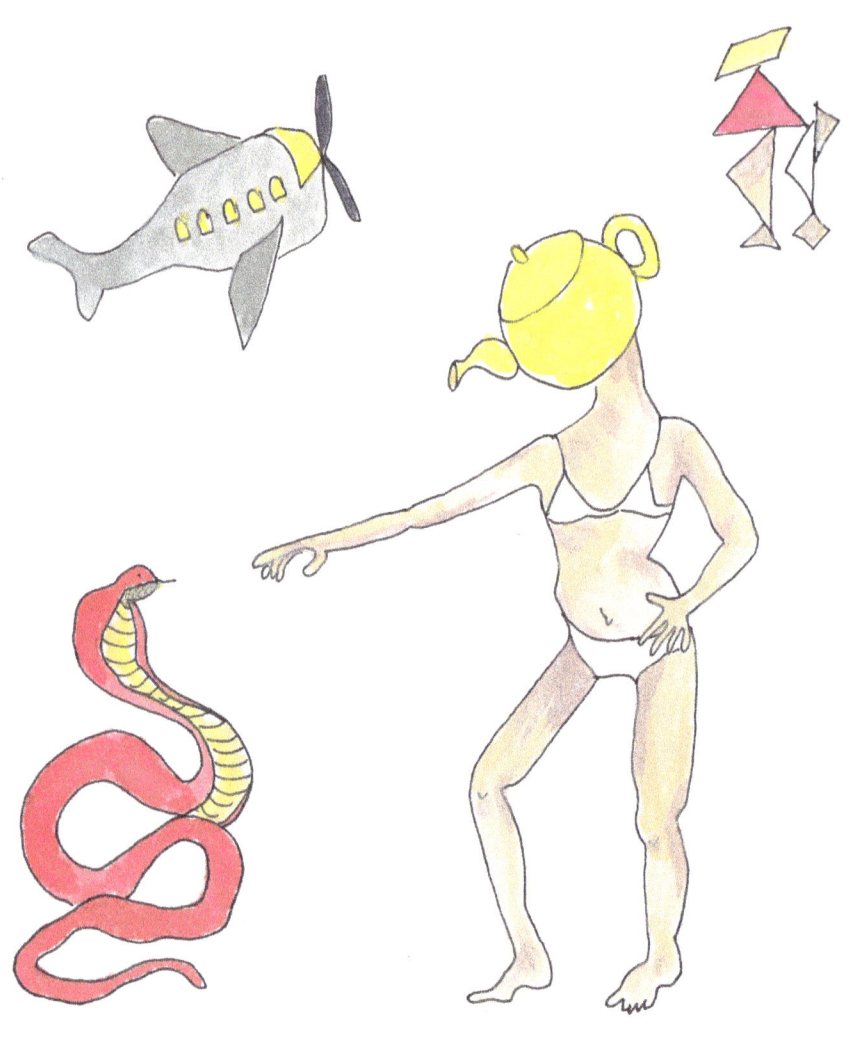

OR I COULD BE SISTER to the DANAÏDES, CONDEMNED as WELL to CARRY WATER in a SIEVE

HOW ALIKE WE SEEM and YET HOW UTTERLY at ODDS

PERHAPS BRICOLAGE HELPS COMPOSE an HOMAGE MOST RESEMBLING the DRUMSONGS of ALL our OLD HEARTS BEATING

HER PET SCHEMES SEEM to ASSUAGE HER SENSE of GUILT, RATHER than to HONOR AUTONOMY

FOR WHOSO GENDERED NOUNS, & OTHER INQUIRIES toward SOLACE

BUT NERO MUST HAVE PLUCKED a CITHARA, for the FIDDLE CAME to BE nearly 1500 YEARS after FLAMES LICKED ROME—SUCH REVERIE

OH, BUT a SINGLE BERRY MIGHT INDUCE a SUITABLE DÉTENTE

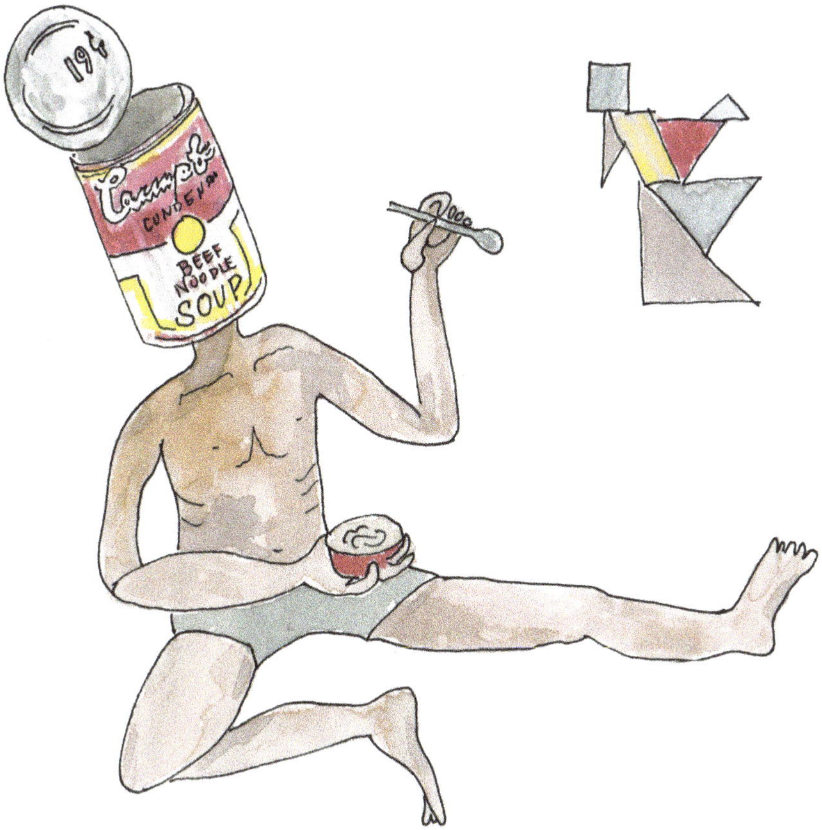

YOU CLAIM NEVER to HAVE PEERED INTO a MIRROR to SEE a CANNIBAL?

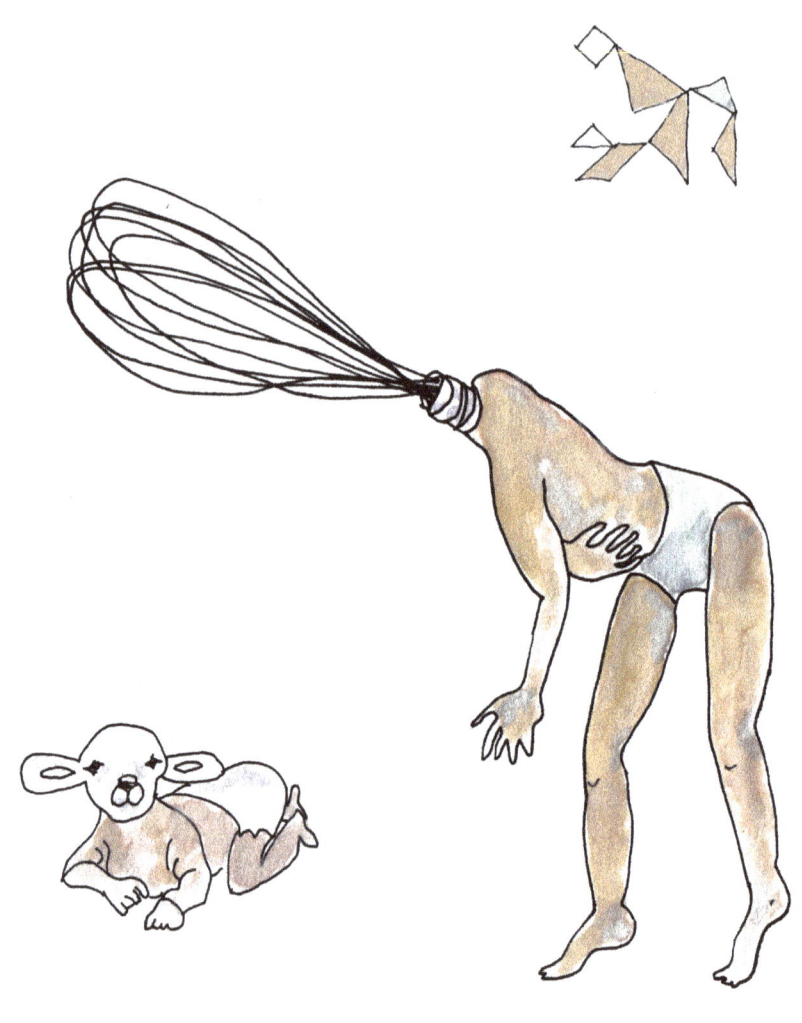

THEIR RECIPE CALLS for TWO CUPS of SNOW, WHISKED with a PINCH of ASHWAGANDHA

III.
GRACE, *an EKPHRASTIC SEQUENCE*

"I want to be famous in the way a pulley is famous,
 a buttonhole, not because it did anything spectacular,
but because it never forgot what it could do."
—*Naomi Shihab Nye*, "Famous"

"… rhyme to the eye is correspondence of parts in pictorial art
or in an infinity of natural things as the two eyes and the two
sides of the body generally, butterfly's wings, paired leaves, shadows
in glass or water."
—*Gerard Manly Hopkins*, (Journals, p. 286)

"Why are there three Graces and why are they sisters? Why do they
hold hands? Why are they smiling, youthful, virginal, wearing a loose
and transparent dress?"
—*Seneca*, "On benefits"

"They throw themselves on the waters of the world, and they know
they will be borne up."
—*Jane Smiley*, A Thousand Acres

"YOU MAY CHOOSE to NAME US WEED or FLOWER, for "WHEN WE DIE, OUR BODIES BECOME the GRASS, and the ANTELOPE EAT the GRASS…"

    (—*after* Mufasa, *from the Lion King &* William Edward Frost, *"L'Allegro," 1848)*

BUT A CAMEL MAY PASS with EASE THROUGH the EYE of A NEEDLE
(—*after* Bertel Thorvaldsen, 1770-1844)

*LET US PAUSE to CONSIDER WHETHER "BYRDES of ON KYNDE &
COLOR FLOK & FLYE ALLWAYES TOGETHER"*
    (—*after* Botticelli, 1445-1510 & William Turner *(The Rescuing of Romish Fox, 1545))*

MYCELIUM, MYCELIUM… the ULTIMATE UNDERWORLD INTERNET
　　(—*after* Peter Paul Rubens, 1636)

DEAR ONE, at TWO MINUTES to MIDNIGHT, YOUR TINCTURE of TIME OFFERS LITTLE CONSOLATION
   (—*after* Raphael, 1483-1520)

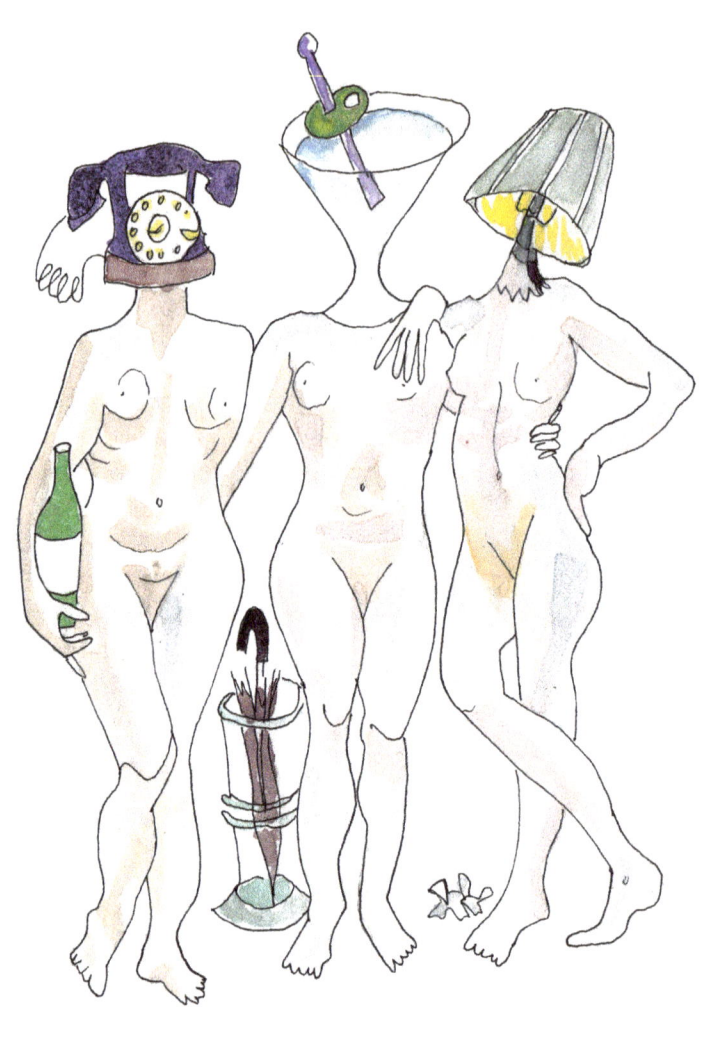

IF ONLY A PICARDY THIRD WERE TONIC for ALL OUR WOES
(—*after* Paul Marie Louis Pierre Richer, c. 1913)

TUCK HER WORDS into a TEAPOT, STEEP for YEARS, READ the LEAVES FOREVER AFTER
      (—*after* Antonio Correggio, *Fresco Camera di San Paolo, Parma, 1519*)

DISPLAYS of FRIPPERY or TRIUMPHS of WILL?
(—*after* Jean Honoré Fragonard, ~1770)

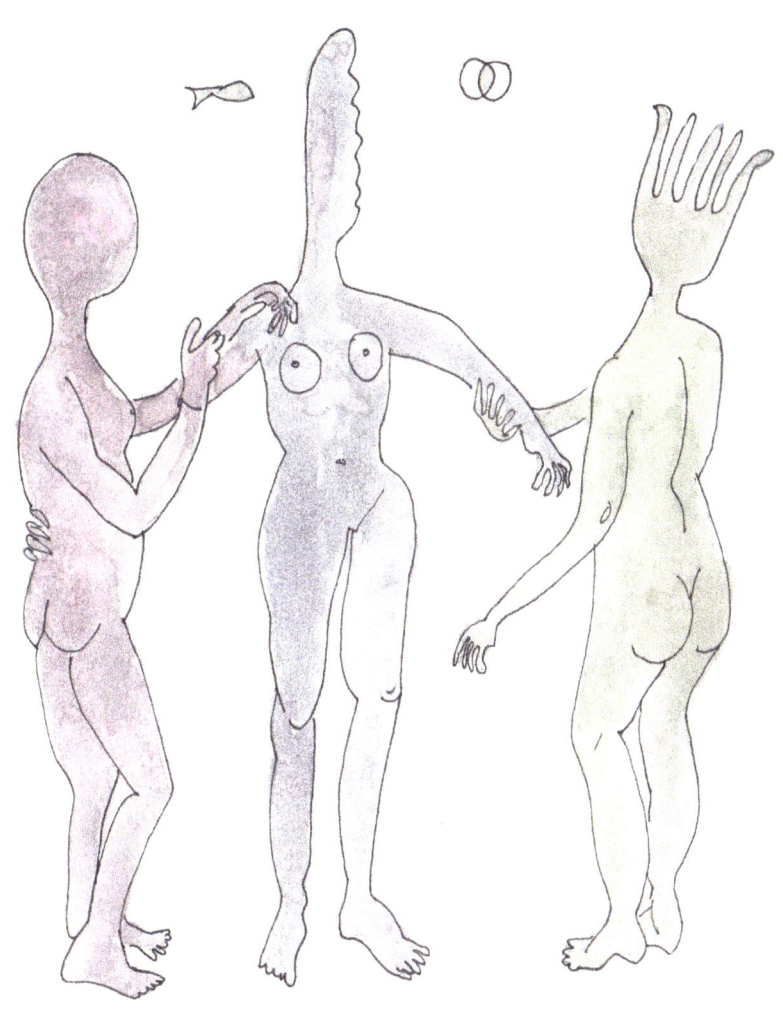

WHEN WE SPEAK of a FINE FETTLE, we DO SO to NOTE YOUR CLEAN EDGES
  (—*after* Charles-André van Loo, -1765)

FRUIT in a BOOT
    (—*after* Chiquita *&* Fruit of the Loom)

SUCH an ALLEGORY of the GIFT ENTREATS EACH to FOLLOW THEIR HEART
    (—after "The Graces Dance," at the Athenian Acropolis ~500 B.C.)

INVISIBLE, INTRICATE, OFTEN UNSUNG OSSICLES
(—*after* Peter Paul Rubens, 1577–1640)

WHICH CONCESSIONS are PALATABLE in this LIGHT of FIREWORKS BLOOMING like AGAPANTHUS?
  (—*after* Sokrates of Boeotia, c 470 BCE)

"NO BALM in GILEAD? NO PHYSICIAN?...IS THERE NO HEALING for the WOUNDS OF MY PEOPLE?"
(—*after* Antonio Canova, 1753-1822 & *Jeremiah* 8 v. 2)

APPARENTLY, OUR SWORDS BEATEN into PLOWSHARES & SPEARS into PRUNINGHOOKS are "READY for PICK-UP"
    (—*after* Hans Baldung Grien, 1484-1545 & *Isaiah 2:4*)

OH, MOTHER DEAR
    (—after "Address in verse to Robert of Anjou, King of Naples," Convenevole da Prato, Tuscany (the 'Regia Carmina'). 1335-c. 1340.)

THROW for BEST of THREE, a DANCE with COMTE de ROCHAMBEAU
    (—*after* William Edward Frost, 1856)

IV.

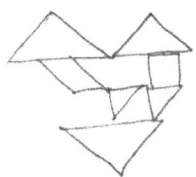

"She is black and white,
Her mane falls wild on her forehead,
And the light breeze moves me to caress her long ear
That is delicate as the skin over a girl's wrist."
       —*James Wright, "A Blessing"*

"The truth isn't always beauty, but the hunger for it is."
       —*Nadine Gordimer*

"So that the truant boy may go steady with the State,
 So that in his spine a memory of wings
 Will make his shoulders tense & bend
 Like a thing already flown
 When the bracelets of another school of love
 Are fastened to his wrists,
 Make a law that doesn't have to wait
 Long until someone comes along to break it."
       —*Larry Levis, "Make a Law So That the Spine
       Remembers Wings"*

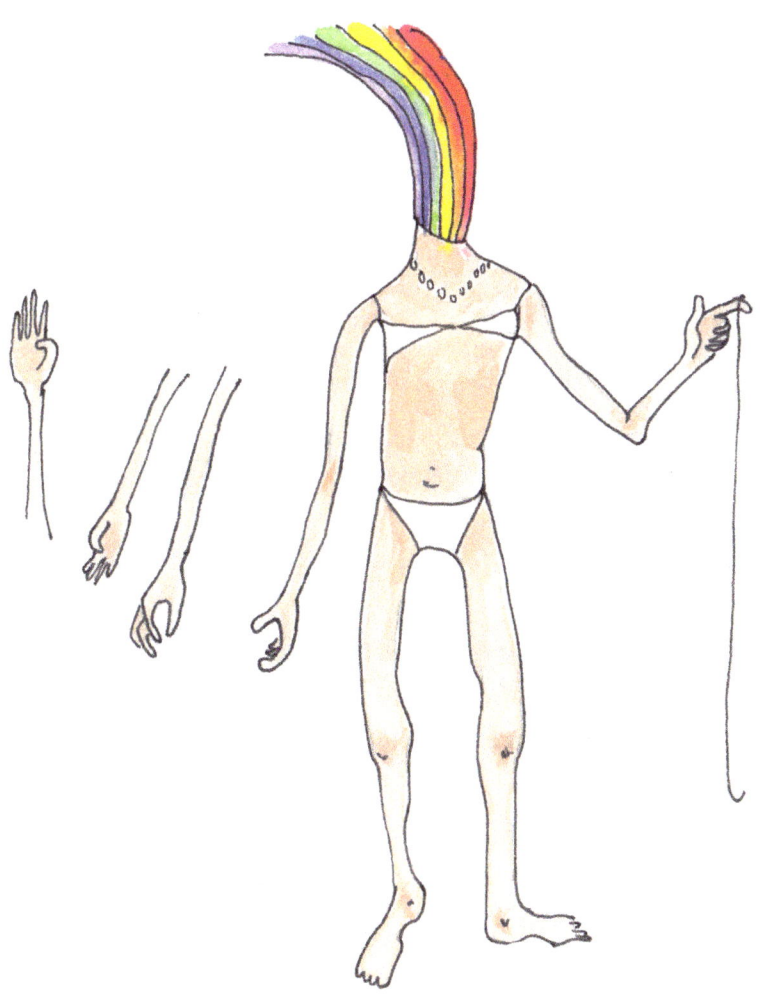

MEMORIA

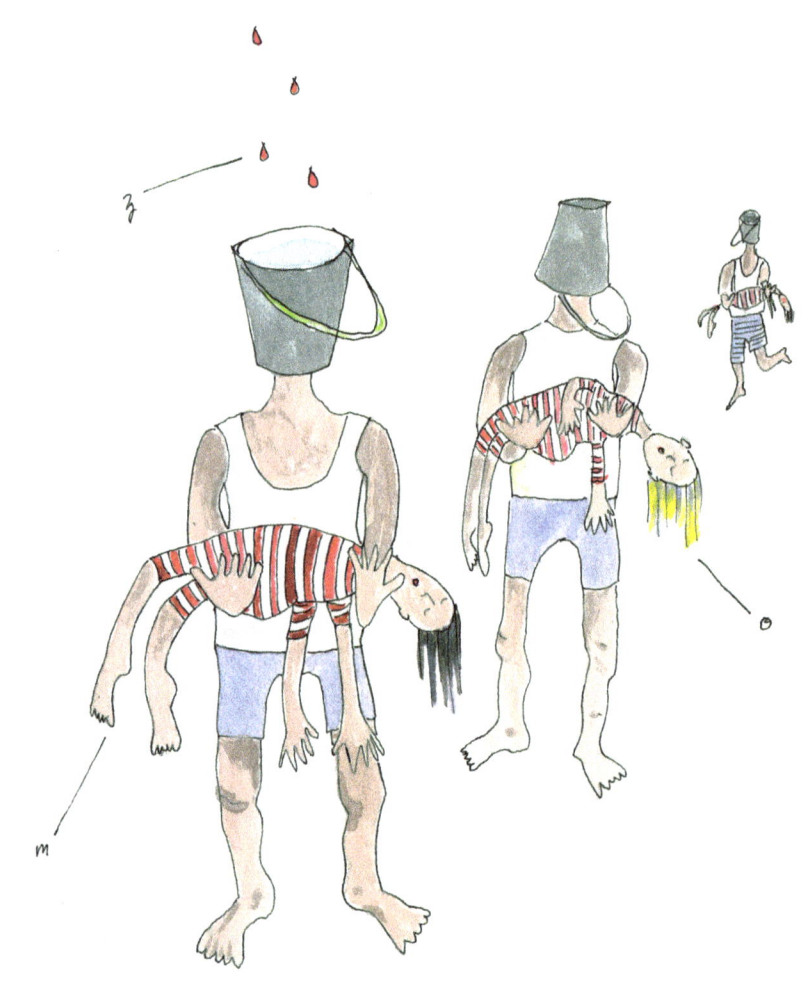

NO PAVILION SUFFICIENTLY VAST

AN ISLAND of ICE RECEDES BEFORE OUR EYES
    (—after a photo by Eric Lefrance/Solent, Olga Strait of Svalbard (Norway))

UTILITY MAY BE a FINE FAITH for THOSE NO LONGER SEEN

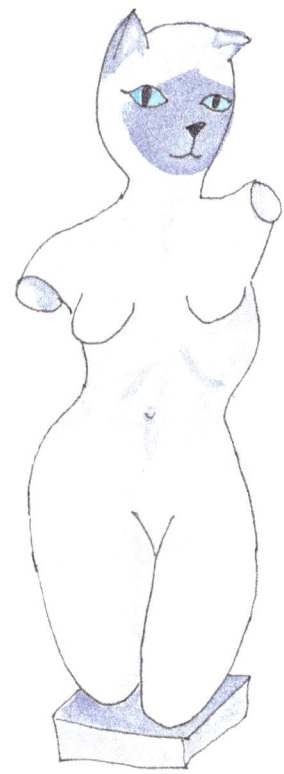

HOW to REIN WILDERNESS, or WILDERNESS REIGNS?

LITTLE RED HOODIE HERESY

SHE HOLDS HER POSE JUST LONG ENOUGH TO INQUIRE:
"ARE YOU—NOBODY—TOO?"
    (—after Emily Dickinson)

CHURCH KEYS or WHATEVER ELSE LETS YOU CRACK OPEN YOUR BELIEF

HOW ORNATE the FUCHSIA BLOSSOMS, WHEN I TENDER THEM SOME CARE

ANTHEM for SUCH PORTALS THROUGH WHICH we USHER OTHERS & for PLACES we CAN TAKE OURSELVES

EKPHRASIS

FOR GIVEN this STRING, I'm DIRIGIBLE

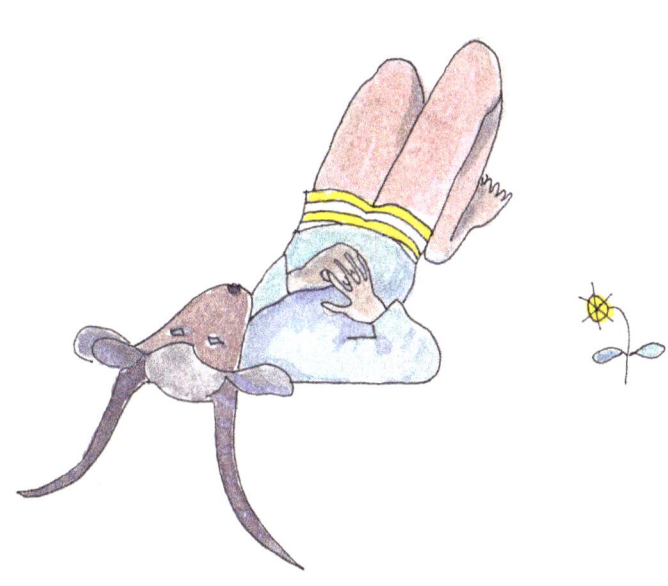

HOW MANY CREATURES STITCH the DEPTHS of LOAM BENEATH SHOULDERS as I CHART the PINNED-UP ANIMALS?

THE GEOMETRY of DESIRE

CERTAINLY, SOMETHING PINIONED RESIDES INSIDE, OPINING, SHOULD YOU CHOOSE to TEASE it OUT

WHERE LANGUAGE MUST ALWAYS FALL SHORT

DIAPHORA

TELL US AGAIN HOW YOU KNOW YOU'RE RIGHT

THERE'S NO ELIXIR LIKE RISK

To EMBRACE the DAY'S GLORY is NOT to DENY EACH ANGUISH

SCHRÖDINGER

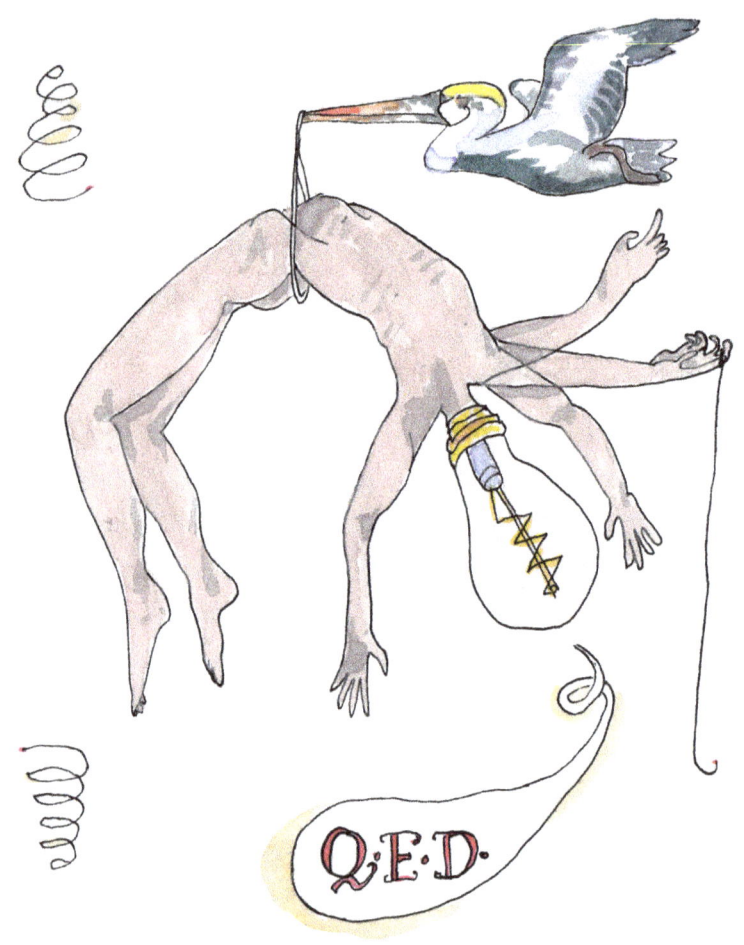

PROOF of GOODWILL'S ARMATURE

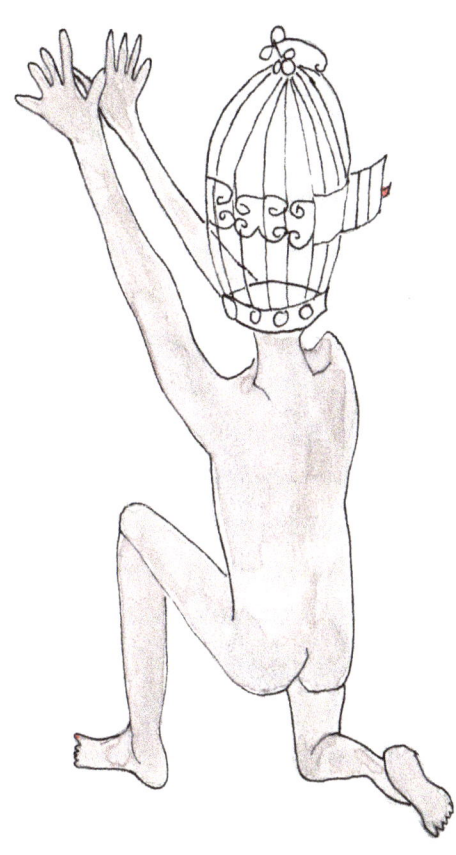

YOU TAKE with YOU EXQUISITE ANSWERS to EVERY QUESTION UNASKED

ACKNOWLEDGMENTS

Appreciation to the editors who've given these poems homes in gorgeous journals & anthologies (sometimes in slightly different versions):

American Journal of Poetry:
    [surely such a beautiful equation should free even...]
    [how ornate the fuchsia blossoms, when i tender them some care]
    [an island of ice recedes before our eyes]
    [whether she's guilty of comparative trauma...]
    [algorithms for insecurity of the food sort]

Brink:
    [you take with you exquisite answers to every question unasked]
    ["no balm in gilead? no physician?... is there no healing..."]
    [dear one, at two minutes to midnight...]

Evergreen: Fairy Tales, Essays, and Fables from the Dark Northwest (Scablands Books):
    [we must rely on lesser circles of protection]
    [little red hoodie heresy]
    [only an ordinance of clouds]
    [for given this string, i'm dirigible]

Ilanot Review, "Picture Issue," nominated for a Pushcart Prize:
    [scalene]
    [memoria]
    [diaphora]
    [ekphrasis]
    [asemic]
    [colosseum]

The Indianapolis Review
    ["please write back soon, sincerely"]
    [how alike we seem and yet how utterly at odds]
    [her pet schemes seem to assuage her sense of guilt...]
    [if stanzas are rooms, downstairs a bear...]
    [perhaps bricolage helps to compose an homage...]

Interim:
    [you may choose to name us weed or flower...]
    [throw for best of three, a dance...]
    [oh, mother dear]
    [displays of frippery or triumphs of will?]

The Journal:
    she holds her pose just long enough...]
    [self-portrait as early-morning cerberus...]
    [church keys or whatever else lets you crack open your belief]
    [there's no elixir like risk]
    [self-portrait as struck match with promethean vixen]
    [to embrace the day's glory is not to deny each anguish]
    [certainly, something pinioned resides inside, opining...]
    [perks to any club come with a price]
    [utility may be a fine faith for those no longer seen]
    [how to rein wilderness, or wilderness reigns?]

Lilac City Fairy Tales Vol. IV, Towers & Dungeons, (Scablands Books)
    [faraday]
    [schrödinger]
    [sanctuary]

Penteract Press Anthology:
    [surely such a beautiful equation should free even...]

Permafrost (finalist for the New Alchemy Award, 2019):
    [you claim never to have peered into a mirror to see a cannibal?]
    [but nero must have plucked a cithara, for the fiddle came to be...]
    [the pacts he breaks might fell an old-growth forest]
    [their recipe calls for two cups of snow, whisked with a pinch of ashwagandha]
    [for whoso gendered nouns, & other inquiries toward solace]
    [oh, but a single berry might induce a suitable détente]
    [or i could be a sister to the danaïdes, condemned as well...]

Poetry Northwest:
    [for whom among us has not felt herself a cipher]
    [our diagram of ubiquitous sorrow]
    [proof of goodwill's armature]
    [an island of trash three times the size of france]

Root & Star:
    [anodyne for everything I've neglected to offer]

Thrush Poetry Journal:
    [superconducting quantum interference devices...]
    [toque pastueño with notation for ultimate sorrow]
    [sobriety suits you]

ヾ(˘ ˘ *)彡

Thank you: Glynnis Fawkes, Mita Mahato, Lauren Haldeman, Maya Jewell Zeller, Camille Dungy, Aimee Nezhukumatathil, Kelli Russell Agodon, Johanna Stoberock, Suzanne Buffam, Ada Limón, Chicu Reddy, Sophie Lucido Johnson, Javier Zabala, M. Acuff, Jennifer Militello, Camille Guthrie, Erika Meitner, Sally Ball, Juan Martinez, Nicole Heffner Callihan, Joy Harjo, Christopher Merrill, Evie Shockley, Alina Stefanescu, Lisa Olstein, Brenda Shaughnessy, Lisa Moore, Julie Choffel, Zoë Ryder White, Henrietta Goodman, Abigail Doan, Kevin Gordon, Brian Turner, Meg Reynolds, Rachel Zucker, Paul Lisicky, Heather Hoffman, Michele Battiste, Jenny Browne, Caitlin McDonnell, Jenn Givhan, Jen Sperry Steinorth, Nick Francis Potter, Lisa Huffaker, Sharon Alker, Emily Somoskey, Libby Miller, and Kynde Kiefel, in particular, among many unnamed others, for helping me navigate toward this work, and for inspiring perhaps without knowing nor with an inkling of intention, yet precisely when needed.

Deepest gratitude: Octavio Quintanilla, Meg Day, Bianca Stone, Terrance Hayes, Kathryn Nuernberger, Kelcey Parker Ervick, Lia Purpura, and Sabrina Orah Mark—my mentor-loves, a genius dream-crew in ferrying *LIKENESS* into the world with generous vision & words; I'm so grateful to have this teeny seat at the kids' table long-bedazzled with the brilliant feast of your works.

Praise: Derek M. Ballard, Evan Robbins, Adam Stark, Björn Miner, "Bartholomew," Eric Varillas, & Z., for keeping things real & for your insights & company on the final stretch.

(●ᴥ●)

Thanks: Leah Huete de Maines, Christen Kincaid, and everyone at Finishing Line Press, for the gift of being seen, and for the treasure of this small beating thing brought to life in full-color between cupped hands. I'm also indebted to writers whose words inform this book, and are included within as epigraphs.

Acknowledgment: Whitman College for support and time; those colleagues who've been buoys during recent storms; exceptional students who've threaded dark waves with phosphorescence.

♡(˚ ֊ ᴥ ֊ ˚)/

Gratitude and love always to Jane Roberts & in memory of H.A. Roberts (1937-2021), much-missed. Ongoing appreciation to Jeremy, for believing in this work & for letting me be lost within it.

Love in all iterations & a side of Voodoo fries: Phineas Teague, Zephyrus Axel, & Thalassa Phoebe, for enduring hope, unequalled joy, & constant inspiration.

(ᴜ•ᴥ•ᴜ)

Enduring appreciation for believing earliest: Sharma Shields, Frances Cannon, Marcela Sulak, Keetje Kuipers, Bill Carty, Helen Vitoria, Morgan Fox, Natalie Solmer, Robert Nazarene, Nina Lohman, Hannah Bonner, Stephanie DeMer, Courtney Mandryk, Claudia Keelan. Thanks to Jenny Molberg, and Kathryn Nuernberger for naming an earlier version of this manuscript Finalist for the *Pleiades Press Visual Poetry Series*. Gratitude to readers at *Permafrost*, who selected seven of the "Tangram" sequence as Finalist for the "New Alchemy Award of 2019," and to all at *The Ilanot Review*, for the Pushcart Prize nomination.

And to you, if you're holding this book: thank you. I wish you all good things. I hope we can work together to try to make things better for our planet, and for all creatures.

PERMISSIONS

Brigit Pegeen Kelly, excerpt from "The Satyr's Heart" from *O Blessed Dark*. Copyright © 2004 by Brigit Pegeen Kelly. Excerpt from "Song" from *Song*. Copyright © 1995 by Brigit Pegeen Kelly. Both reprinted with the permission of The Permissions Company, LLC on behalf of BOA Editions, Ltd. All rights reserved.

Larry Levis, excerpt from "Make a Law So That the Spine Remembers Wings" from *The Darkening Trapeze: Last Poems*. Copyright © 2014 by Larry Levis. Reprinted with the permission of The Permissions Company, LLC on behalf of Graywolf Press, www.graywolfpress.org.

Wesley McNair, excerpt from "The Unfastening" from *The Unfastening*. Copyright © 2017 by Wesley McNair. Reprinted with the permission of The Permissions Company, LLC on behalf of David R Godine, Publisher, Inc., www.godine.com.

Naomi Shihab Nye, excerpt from "Famous" from *Words Under the Words: Selected Poems*. Copyright © 1995 by Naomi Shihab Nye. Used with the permission of Far Corner Books.

Charles Simic, excerpt from "Stone" from *Selected Early Poems*. Copyright © 1999 by Charles Simic. Reprinted with the permission of George Braziller, Inc. (New York), www.georgebraziller.com. All rights reserved.

James Wright, excerpt from "A Blessing" from *Above the River: The Complete Poems and Selected Prose*. Copyright 1990 by James Wright. Reprinted by permission of Wesleyan University Press.

Thank you, Frederick Courtright.

(=^ I ^=)

Katrina Roberts is the author of *Underdog; Friendly Fire; The Quick; How Late Desire Looks,* and *Lace.* She edited the anthology *Because You Asked: A Book of Answers on the Art & Craft of the Writing Life.* Her poems have been included in *The Pushcart Prize Anthology, Best American Poetry, The Bread Loaf Anthology of New American Poets,* and elsewhere. Her visual erasures and reviews, poetry comics, and graphic pieces appear widely in journals such as *BOMB, Brink, Interim, The Ilanot Review, Thrush, American Journal of Poetry, Root & Star, Poetry Northwest, Permafrost, The Journal,* and in anthologies including *Evergreen: Fairy Tales, Essays, and Fables from the Dark Northwest.* She writes and draws in Walla Walla, Washington, where she tends to vines and animals; teaches, and curates the Visiting Writers Reading Series at Whitman College; and co-runs Tytonidae Cellars & the Walla Walla Distilling Company. (www.katrinaroberts.net & IG: @kittybucket)

Afterword

We live in a complicated world—Katrina Roberts, in *LIKENESS*, knows this, too, and reflects it in the structures she fashions on the page.
The "Prologue" is shaped like a house, for instance. You'll see
a roof, a window, and a foundation sitting on air.
This house that reads like a prologue will forever float in the middle of the page.
Forever.
Unless you draw yourself as a struck match and burn it down.
Then the smoke and ash will fill the white air of the page.
Forever. Unless...
And how to enter a house, this work asks, in which a mirror becomes a window?
Wouldn't you first have to see the window and then climb through to see
that it's a mirror? And then, how to enter the mirror?
To what becoming will it lead you?
Once inside the house, do you yourself become the mirror?
What will you reflect back to the world?
Will you show the true likeness to the things we think we are not?
You have a broom's brush for a head.
A hammer.
A bird.
You are a visual utterance.
Your eye is a mouth. Your mouth, an eye.
But only if the world chooses to see itself in you. To hear you.
To be an ekphrasis of who you are. Only if it chooses not to tear, word by word, this house of images Katrina has built.
After all, Katrina's house is made of images. And words.
And the images have a likeness to words and the words have a likeness to images.
Such as, "She looks like a an early-morning Cerberus and she looks into the mirror and the mirror looks back at her and her *looking* is full of pleasure."
Or, "The bats with human bodies dangle from what looks to be a tree branch and speak to each other in their own language."
This work will lead you to ask: Will the mirrors remain intact?
And if broken, what, then, will be reflected?
And isn't our own house also made of words? And images? Our lives?
What does this say about our vulnerability? Is this what makes us all alike?
There must be a name for this equation.
A set of words, a set of images.
Which is to say, how to frame a book with language when the contents of the book seem to resist it? To what likeness could it be compared?
"This *likeness* is like this *likeness*."
Will the likeness ever tell us what it truly means?
Will it bleed?
As if to say, "We are more than alphabet, more than sound, more than what we read."

—*Octavio Quintanilla*

Is this what we look like to others—pieced together from precious, found parts? Blazing with tender color and light? Dancing and keening and contemplating? Oh, all the ways, unseen and unknown, we hold ourselves, project our desires, protect our interiors—captured in the pages of this glorious and magical collection. Hieroglyphic (but entirely legible), alchemical (but in no way esoteric) the drawing/word conversations in *LIKENESS* are made of the stuff of anyone's day: here is a hammer, a rabbit, a birdcage…and here we all are, bodied in grief, in yearning, in joy, our dreams bearing forth older, deeper forms of knowing. "For whom among us has not felt herself a cipher," Katrina Roberts writes. With these words as your guide, enter this most fabulous and fabular world.

—Lia Purpura

I want to use these wonderful meta-fables and homemade fairy tales as poetry prompts. My poem after Katrina Roberts' [you claim never to have peered into a mirror to see a cannibal?], for example, might involve a soup can or mention the pen & ink quirks of Andy Warhol. *LIKENESS* is a veritable inspiration engine. Even the table of contents reads like a brilliant cento of poetry. In fact, I doubt Roberts distinguishes writing and drawing: every sumptuous line is a poem.

—Terrance Hayes

What curious wilderness might come from allowing the visual to occupy more fully the space of text—lest we've forgotten, too, that text is visual? In *LIKENESS*, Roberts is both auger & answer. At once a prophecy of potential for the flexibility of language & fresh confirmation of the fact of our own imaginations, these poems are unconfined & still razor-sharp in their generosity. I have waited for a collection like this. *LIKENESS* is a thrilling & necessary addition to our understanding of multiplicity & its joy.

—Meg Day

If, as Max Ernst said, the art of collage creates "a spark of poetry," Katrina Roberts's *LIKENESS* is an utter explosion of poetry. *LIKENESS* is a book of bodies, machines, explosions, and equations. In these pages, Roberts urgently attempts to solve the mystery of the mortal body through immortal bodies: sketches of sculptures, drawings of paintings, and speech bubbles filled with signs, signifiers, and scribbles. The bodies in *LIKENESS*, drawn with straightforward, inviting lines and painted with loose and lively color, have heads of animals, kitchen utensils, weapons, and rainbows. The imagery calls to mind the haunted energy of Bianca Stone or Louise Bourgeois, but the singular vision is all Roberts.

—Kelcey Parker Ervick

LIKENESS reminds me of Donald Winnicott saying of Francis Bacon, "in looking at faces he seems to need to be painfully striving towards being seen, which is at the basis of creative looking." Roberts's "faces" and portraits are disfigured with the ordinary objects of our everyday piecing together lyrical vignettes of Life. What I love best about these delightful creatures is that they show us the humor and tragedy of our own heads: songs of the psyche, in bright and colorful poised solace, carrying and embracing one another. This is a gorgeous and enchanting book.

—Bianca Stone

Animal-headed humans and human-bodied animals speak to each other in mathematical equations, alchemical symbols, and asemic languages. Such are the surprises and delights of poems in Katrina Roberts's *LIKENESS*. Come revel in the surreal abundance of the world teeming with extraordinary beings, becomings, transformations, and unlikely relationships. Roberts's perceptive eye teaches us image by image, poem by poem, how disparate fragments can be drawn together into a wonderfully strange and beautifully perceptive whole. These poetry comics reinvent the lyric mood and reveal the transformative power of imagery and metaphor. *LIKENESS* is a pleasure to behold that teaches you, with each passing page, how to see the world with fresh wondering eyes.

—Kathryn Nuernberger

Katrina Roberts' *LIKENESS* is unlike any book or cloud or sorrow or sanctuary or house or stone or garment or forest or revelry or snowstorm or body or star or needle or lullaby I have ever been inside. It is far more beautiful. And far more real.

—*Sabrina Orah Mark*

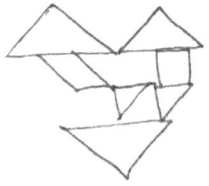

www.ingramcontent.com/pod-product-compliance
Lightning Source LLC
Chambersburg PA
CBHW042138160426
43200CB00020B/2980